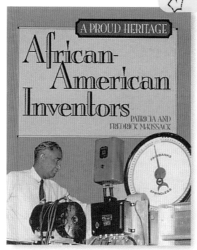

"I squealed for joy!" That's what children's book author Patricia C. McKissack said when she heard that a picture book she wrote was going to be published. The book, *Flossie and the Fox*, describes how Flossie, a young African American girl in the South, outsmarts a sly fox.

Patricia has written over one hundred books. Most of her books are about African Americans. For example, she wrote *African-American Inventors* to show that many things people use today were invented by African Americans.

"I write because there's a need to have books for, by, and about the African American experience and how we helped to develop this country," Patricia said.

Patricia McKissack was born on August 9, 1944, in Smyrna, Tennessee. Her family moved to St. Louis, Missouri, when she was three years old. After her parents divorced, she stayed in St. Louis with her grandparents, her father's parents. Her mother, brother, and sister moved back to Tennessee. Patricia moved back to Tennessee when she was twelve and lived with her other grandparents, her mother's parents.

On hot summer nights in Tennessee, she and her family would sit on the front porch. They would listen to people tell stories. Her grandmother would tell scary stories. Her mother would recite poems or tell stories she knew. Her grandfather would tell stories about his childhood and about the family's ancestors. Patricia loved listening to these stories.

Smyrna, Tennessee

Just Like Patricia McKissack

by Clary L. Donaldson

Harcourt

SCHOOL PUBLISHERS

Cover, ©Public Domain/Education Department/JFK Presidential Library and Museum; p.3, p.13, ©Harcourt Telescope; p.4, ©Town of Smyrna, Tennessee; p.5, ©Joanna McCarthy/The Image Bank/ Getty Images; p.6, ©David R. Frazier Photolibrary, Inc./Alamy; p.7, ©Ragnar Schmuck/fStop/Getty Images; p.8, ©BananaStock/SuperStock; p.9, ©Hulton Archive/Getty Images; p.10, ©CORR/AFP/ Getty Images; p.11, ©Library of Congress Prints & Photographs Division; p.12, ©Harcourt, Inc.; Association for Library Services for Children/American Library Association/Harcourt, Inc.; p.14, ©Robert Manella/Iconica/Getty Images.

Printed in China

ISBN 10: 0-15-351532-5
ISBN 13: 978-0-15-351532-3

Ordering Options
ISBN 10: 0-15-351214-0 (Grade 4 Advanced Collection)
ISBN 13: 978-0-15-351214-8 (Grade 4 Advanced Collection)
ISBN 10: 0-15-358122-0 (package of 5)
ISBN 13: 978-0-15-358122-9 (package of 5)

5 6 7 8 9 10 985 12 11 10 09

Listening to these wonderful storytellers was very important to Patricia. "Long before I became a writer, I was a listener and observer," she said. By listening to and observing these skilled storytellers, Patricia learned how to tell a story. Listening also helped her study how good storytellers use words and describe characters. Though she didn't realize it at the time, all of those nights on the front porch in the summer were helping Patricia become a strong and skilled author.

Those stories had a great influence on Patricia in another way. Often her grandfather would use the names of Patricia and her brother and sister in the stories he told. The characters in those stories were always brave and smart, so Patricia and her siblings grew up feeling confident.

When she was about seven years old, Patricia began to love reading. She once said, "To me, reading is like breathing; both are essential."

Patricia attended Tennessee State University in Nashville, Tennessee. While a student there, she ran into a young man named Fred. They had known each other when they were children. Patricia and Fred began to date, and they were married in 1964. That same year, Patricia graduated from college with a degree in English literature. She also obtained a certificate that allowed her to be a schoolteacher. Patricia and Fred had three children: Frederick, Robert, and John.

Patricia knew from the time she was in college that she wanted to be a writer. However, raising three children kept her quite busy. Though she didn't write any books at that time in her life, she did some important work that prepared her for her career as a writer.

One way Patricia prepared to be an author was to spend time in the public library. There, she read many children's books. She studied how the authors wrote books that children could easily read and understand. She studied how the authors chose topics that would interest children. She looked at catalogs of books that were for sale. The catalogs helped her see what kinds of books publishers liked to publish and sell.

Patricia also read many book reviews. When an author writes a new book, another writer often writes his or her opinion of the book. This book review is then printed in a newspaper or magazine. Reading book reviews helped Patricia understand what kinds of books people liked and also what kinds of books people *didn't* like.

Patricia said, "The library was my lifesaver. Besides being free, air-conditioned, and quiet, it was a wonderful place to learn my trade."

Patricia was able to work outside the home as her children grew older. She taught junior high and high school English for nine years. Then she earned a master's degree. When a person earns a master's degree, it means they are very knowledgeable about a certain subject. Patricia's master's degree was in children's literature.

Later she became a children's book editor. Editors help authors improve the books they have written. Patricia worked as an editor for six years. "My career as a teacher helped me recognize what books were needed and what children enjoyed reading; my career as an editor taught me how to develop an idea," Patricia said.

Paul Laurence Dunbar

One day, Fred asked Patricia, "If you could do anything you want to do in the whole wide world for the rest of your life, what would you do?"

"Write books," Patricia answered.

"Okay, let's do that," said Fred. "We'll take it as far as we can go. We'll take it day by day."

Patricia began her career as a full-time children's book author. She wrote her first book about an African American poet named Paul Dunbar. Patricia's grandmother had enjoyed reciting Dunbar's poems. That book is titled *Paul Laurence Dunbar: A Poet to Remember.*

Fred often helps Patricia with her books. If Patricia wants to write a book about a famous person, Fred does a lot of the research for it. This means that he finds all the information he can in books and magazines. He gives all of this information to Patricia. Then Patricia writes the manuscript. The manuscript is the rough draft of a book. Patricia gives her rough draft to Fred. He checks to make sure that all of the information in the draft is accurate. He makes some changes and suggestions. Then he hands the rough draft back to Patricia. The rough draft goes back and forth like this until both Patricia and Fred are happy with it. Then they send the manuscript to a publisher and hope that it gets published.

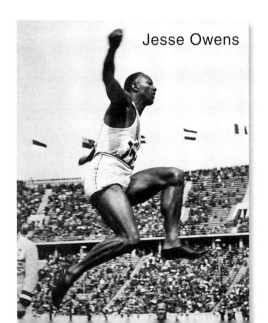
Jesse Owens

Zora Neale Hurston

Patricia gets many of her ideas for books from African American history. She wrote about important African Americans, such as the speedy, graceful runner Jesse Owens who participated in the 1936 Summer Olympic Games. She wrote about the brilliant civil rights leader Martin Luther King, Jr. She wrote about the great storyteller Zora Neale Hurston.

Patricia gets ideas for stories in many ways. She gets ideas from the places where she and Fred travel. She gets ideas from the people they meet. Patricia keeps a diary. In the diary, she may describe mischievous children or unique adults she has met. She may describe exotic places she has visited. These ideas may later become part of the books she writes.

Coretta Scott King Award

Some writers begin to write a story without knowing what will happen next in the story, or how the story will end. Patricia, though, does not write fiction stories in this way. "When I'm writing fiction, I think the book through first. I walk around with a manuscript in my head for a year or sometimes longer until I have very clearly in my mind a beginning, a middle, and an end."

Patricia's method clearly works because she has won the Coretta Scott King Award numerous times. The award is given to African American authors who write outstanding books. One of her books was also named a Newbery Honor Book.

One of the illustrators that Patricia worked with has also won the Coretta Scott King Award. His name is Jerry Pinkney. Jerry Pinkney won this award five times! One of these awards was for the illustrations in Patricia's book, *Goin' Someplace Special.* This book is about Patricia's wonderful memories of going to the public library in Nashville, Tennessee.

Patricia and Fred are very involved in the illustrations for their books. They do a lot of research and travel to different places to be sure that they give the illustrators as much information as possible. For example, when Patricia wrote a book about plantations called *Christmas in the Big House, Christmas in the Quarters*, she and Fred visited a plantation in Virginia. They found out about everything from the food the people ate to how they did their chores.

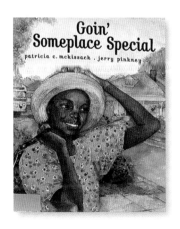

Today, Patricia and Fred live in the town of Chesterfield, Missouri, which is just outside of St. Louis. They continue to write books "to enlighten, to change attitudes, to set goals, and to build bridges." Patricia is pleased that her many books have helped others understand African American culture. "I write because there is a clear need for books written about the minority experience in America," Patricia says. Though her books are written about African Americans, she says she "writes for children of all races."

Think Critically

1. List two facts and two opinions stated in this book.

2. Why do you think the author wrote this book?

3. How did the storytellers in Patricia's family help her become a writer?

4. What word means almost the same thing as *brilliant* does on page 11?

5. What are some details from this book that interested you?

 Art

Make an Illustration Choose a scene from one of Patricia McKissack's books and create your own illustration for it.

School-Home Connection Share this story with a family member. Then have a discussion about how families can influence people's career choices.

Word Count: 1,455(1,469)